LEGAL WRITING
and the
LONE RANGER

Every Lawyer Has a Silver Bullet

DANIEL J. KORNSTEIN

authorHOUSE®

AuthorHouse™
1663 Liberty Drive
Bloomington, IN 47403
www.authorhouse.com
Phone: 833-262-8899

This book is a work of non-fiction. Unless otherwise noted, the author and the publisher
make no explicit guarantees as to the accuracy of the information contained in this book
and in some cases, names of people and places have been altered to protect their privacy.

Published by AuthorHouse 09/29/2020

ISBN: 978-1-6655-0197-2 (sc)
ISBN: 978-1-6655-0180-4 (e)

Print information available on the last page.

Any people depicted in stock imagery provided by Getty Images are models,
and such images are being used for illustrative purposes only.
Certain stock imagery © Getty Images.

This book is printed on acid-free paper.

CONTENTS

PREFACE

EVERY LAWYER'S SILVER BULLET

Okay, so you graduated from law school. That doesn't impress me much. Lots of people go to law school. The real question for today is: Can you write? Lawyers have a professional obligation to become the best writers they can be.

I started to think about legal writing from a new angle when I read about the death in 1999 of Clayton Moore, the actor who most famously played the fictional masked "Lone Ranger" on 1950s television.

For those too young to recall that popular weekly cowboy program, the hero — one of the legendary lawmen known as Texas Rangers — was the sole survivor of an ambush by a gang of outlaws. Seriously wounded, the surviving Ranger was found and nursed back to health by a Native American named Tonto. From then on, the Lone Ranger and what the (now politically incorrect) television announcer called "his faithful Indian companion" Tonto roamed the American Old West looking, like an energetic public interest law firm, for wrongs to right and villains to bring to justice.

At the end of each episode, the grateful townspeople would ask, "Who was that masked man?" Then one of them would find a silver bullet intentionally left there, and they would instantly know the identity of their hero. The silver bullet was the Lone Ranger's calling card, his signature, his trademark.

The Lone Ranger's silver bullet calling card was symbolic and should resonate with lawyers. A silver bullet is a metaphor for a simple, seemingly magical solution to a difficult problem. The Lone Ranger decided to use bullets forged from the precious metal as a symbol of justice, law and order, and to remind himself and others that life has value and the decision to shoot someone is not to be taken lightly. The Lone Ranger explained that he does not shoot to kill, but instead tried to disarm his opponent as painlessly as possible and then let the law dispense justice. His silver bullets were symbols of justice.

For lawyers, the Lone Ranger is more than an antiquated pop cultural reference. An enduring icon, the Lone Ranger had his "silver bullet," and we lawyers have ours: our legal writing. The Lone Ranger made his silver bullets from a friend's secret silver mine; we lawyers make our writing from our own personal mine of training, practice, talent, style, and imagination. Our legal writing is a simple, seemingly magical solution to a difficult problem, our calling card, our legitimate advertising, our signature, our trademark, our fingerprint, our identity card. We become known by our legal writing.

Handcrafted silver bullets are too much work for some people, when machine-tooled base lead can do the job. It is the same with legal writing. Most lawyers have at least some talent as writers, but it takes time and practice for a lawyer to learn to write well. And good legal writers want to leave a calling card. They want it to be distinctive and good and memorable. The writing is you.

How many times have we judged our adversaries or colleagues — for good or bad — by the caliber (!) and quality of their legal writing? Often. We get served with an impressive set of motion papers and we remember it. We see a lousy set and our opinion of the lawyer drops accordingly. We receive an excellent, persuasive brief, one with style and panache, and we show it around. Maybe we ask ourselves: Why can't we write a brief like that? The answer is: You can.

The lawyer is at heart a writer. The life of the lawyer is at its core a literary one. "I think the law should be a literary profession," said the late Supreme Court Justice Ruth Bader Ginsburg. "The best legal practitioners do regard law as an art as well as a craft."

Lawyers write. Lawyers use words. We write briefs, memos, letters, legal opinions. Words are our tools, and wielding the written word is the lawyer's most effective weapon. The lawyer's principal working tool is the

English language, in all its potential expressive glory. Writing is the main way we do our job.

Writing is what we do, it is how we function, and all of us should want to do it better. We want to express our thoughts in compelling language. We fuss about style. We want to make our points more clearly, more elegantly; we want our writing to be appreciated, to be more effective, and, ultimately, more persuasive. When we write well, we capture the attention of our audience much better than when we write poorly. We take pains to be simple, clear and succinct.

Every lawyer, from seasoned veteran to summer associate, from tenured law professor to first-year law student, can improve that tool and sharpen that writing weapon. We can take advantage of the ineffable loveliness of the English language, mobilize it, and send it into legal battle. We can weaponize words.

But how? Good writing is hard work, and the act of writing, like any creative act, will always be enveloped in a strong element of mystery. Good writing is the hardest form of thinking. Bad writing comes from bad thinking. Good legal writing requires patience and discipline. It involves the agony of turning profoundly difficult and abstract thoughts into lucid and persuasive and tight-fitting language, making those thoughts visible and clear. If the writing is good, then the result seems effortless and inevitable.

Some helpful hints — silver bullets, if you will — exist. The following suggestions are not just subjective matters of individual style or literary taste. Objective reasons explain why some writing is better than other writing. I say "hints" and "suggestions" rather than "rules" for a reason. Formal "rules" imply and emphasize, in a highly dogmatic way, a straitjacket, a hard and fast limit to what can be done. Legal writing is not so mechanical. Just as when occasionally you like red wine with fish for it to taste better, sometimes you need to break "rules" to write better.

On the other hand, the suggestions here are necessarily somewhat selective and idiosyncratic. This short book is my chance to share with you, for your own use, some of what I like, what I admire, and what I do. I chose my own guidelines and focused on issues I most often come across. Others may disagree. Fewer absolutes govern legal writing than you think.

These suggestions are aimed specifically at legal writing style, although many of the ideas apply to expository writing in general. But this is not a primer on grammar or punctuation or everyday usage. For those subjects, you will have to look elsewhere. Many such stylebooks exist; this is a little book about legal writing.

But good legal writing is not learned from a guidebook, no matter how excellent. You don't learn how to play golf by reading a book on golf; you don't learn how to swim by reading a guidebook; you don't learn how to make love by reading a marriage manual. You learn by doing. So too the only way to learn good legal writing is by writing.

No single stylebook can tell you everything you want to know about legal writing. A distinctive legal writing style is not perfected by memorizing and woodenly following a list of rules, no matter how excellent or how entertainingly laid out. It would be just as silly to think that giving someone a copy of Strunk & White's iconic *Elements of Style* will automatically earn that person a Pulitzer Prize as it would be to imagine that familiarity with the following guidelines by itself will turn a lawyer into a Holmes, a Cardozo, or a Brandeis — or, from more recent examples, a Scalia or a Kagan.

Legal writing is important. It is important to me and should be to you. Please understand the collegial spirit in which these "tips" are given. They are not a straitjacket. They are simply meant to encourage care, creativity, and persuasiveness. They are one shirtsleeve lawyer's notions — accumulated like barnacles from sailing through the sometimes rough seas of almost fifty years of litigation practice — of what makes for good legal writing, a personal view (by a lawyer who cares deeply about writing) of what works best, what is most effective. I think they are useful; I try myself to follow them.

But you may have a different personal vision, your own style. My style might not be yours. Just as we may differ in choosing our favorite authors or favorite foods, so too we may have different tastes in what makes for effective legal writing. Great. Your ideas may be better. You may forge more powerful and effective silver writing bullets. Good luck. The results are what count.

The personality of the lawyer should cling to what he or she writes. The advocate's personality has a role and should not be wholly suppressed. Style, Justice Holmes once wrote, "is the personal equation of the writer." Going on, Holmes added, "when the style is fully formed, if it has a sweet undersong, we call it beautiful, and the writer may do what he likes with words, or syntax; the material is plastic in his hands to image himself, which is all that anyone can give."

This volume is slim, which has its own attraction. Slim volumes have a magic about them, a purity that tingles. Fat volumes may have heft and majesty, but rarely do they tingle. I hope this little book tingles for you.

In any event, with optimism and shared professional values, with a love of both law and the English language, and in the sincere belief that you too care about legal writing, I pass these ideas, suggestions, and pieces of advice on to you.

ONE

ARE YOU GUILTY OF BAD WRITING?

Lawyers' writing has been long been the object of criticism, ridicule, and derision. If you think the quality of your legal writing is unimportant, think again. An article from the March 4, 2004 New York Times should change your mind. In that article, entitled "Judge Finds a Typo-Prone Lawyer Guilty of Bad Writing," reporter Adam Liptak wrote that "courts are becoming increasingly impatient with many lawyers' substandard writing skills."

Liptak described a case in which a federal judge reduced an attorney's fee request because the attorney's legal papers "were infested with typographical errors." The judge went on to describe the lawyer's prose as "vague, ambiguous, unintelligible, verbose and repetitive." And this was in a fee application!

The same article also reported on a different case in which a judge "chastised another lawyer for textual malfeasance." The judge criticized the lawyer in that case for his "unrestrained and unnecessary use of the bold, underline, and 'all caps' functions of word processing or his repeated use of exclamation marks to emphasize points in his briefs." Such techniques, continued the judge, "really amount to a written form of shouting" and "are simply inappropriate" in a brief.

Bad writing can lose a strong case because the court may not see your strong case. Courts have reinforced the need for effective writing by imposing sanctions for verbosity, lack of organization, and errors in grammar and citations.

"Bad writing does not normally warrant sanctions, but we draw the line at gibberish." That is how the Seventh Circuit ended a 2019 opinion in which the Court of Appeals ordered a lawyer to show cause why he should not be sanctioned for a bad appeal brief.

In a 2016 interview with the *National Law Journal*, Judge Richard Posner criticized judges for bad writing, and his criticisms apply to lawyers as well. Posner urged us to avoid "stale, opaque, confusing jargon" and "terminological complexity." He stressed the use of "ordinary day-to-day language." We may disagree with some of Posner's crotchets, but we can't disagree with his overall criticism.

And then of course we have the classic 1937 cutting comment from the late, witty Yale law professor Fred Rodell. "There are two things wrong with almost all legal writing," lamented Rodell. "One is its style. The other is its content." Now that's what I call good, pungent, pithy writing.

In short, modern legal writing is full of bad habits. Law schools, unfortunately, scant the subject. Even where it is offered, a superficial legal research writing course for one term in the first year of law school is not enough. And law firms are too busy meeting court deadlines to properly train young lawyers how to write better. As a result, bad legal writing habits persist and spread by imitation. We are making dull the tools of our trade.

One cannot change all this in a moment, but one can at least work on and change one's own habits. The situation can be improved if one is willing to take the necessary trouble.

If you think this little book has no value, then stop here. If you are sure your legal writing is perfect and cannot be improved, close this book and do something else. But if you think your legal writing has room for improvement, if you do not want to be found guilty of bad writing or "textual malfeasance," if you want to avoid "stale, opaque, confusing, jargon," if you want to escape Fred Rodell's withering criticism, read on. And if you are now guilty of bad writing, if you must own up to "textual malfeasance," and want to know what you are doing wrong and be rehabilitated, read on.

TWO

THE STARTING POINT: WIDE READING

Good legal writing starts with good writing, and good writing begins with wide reading. To write well, read voraciously and omnivorously. Those who constantly read tend to write coherently. Physically we are what we eat, but mentally we are what we read, and what we read becomes the model for how we write. Read good writers, and your own writing will show it. Our writing style builds on writing we like. So read, and read some more, and not just law.

"You can't be a good writer," says J.K. Rowling, author of the Harry Potter books, "without being a devoted reader." And Nobel Prize-winner William Faulkner once said that anyone who wants to be a writer should be a reader first: "Read, read, read everything – trash, classics, good and bad, and see how they do it. Just like a carpenter who works as an apprentice and studies the master. Read!"

"The best teachers of writing," says Chief Justice John Roberts, "are good writers who you read, and you kind of absorb it when you read them.... You develop a lot as a writer the more you read.... The only way to be a good writer is to be a good reader."

Your non-legal reading, both fiction and nonfiction, should not stop, as it sadly too often does, when you graduate from college. Reading is the great equalizer, today's intellectual equivalent of what the Colt 45 revolver was in the Wild West. Just as Argentinian author Jorge Luis Borges famously created a vast imaginary "Library of Babel," I imagine what I call a mythical University of Books for Free Continuing Education, where admission is open to anyone and is more valuable in reality than the most prestigious and expensive academic degree.

Read constantly, read all the time, because it is impossible to acquire a rich, full sense of language without reading plenty of good literature, nonfiction as well as fiction. Some of the best writers write nonfiction.

Who are your favorite fiction and nonfiction writers? Marcel Proust, Henry James, and Joseph Conrad are great writers, but their often long and convoluted sentences in paragraphs that go on for pages might not be the best models for writing good legal briefs. For that purpose, the clearer, simpler, more straightforward, more easily understood writing of Ernest Hemingway, Rudyard Kipling, Somerset Maugham, John McPhee, Roger Angell, and V.S. Naipaul yields better examples. Being understood is, after all, the first goal of legal writing.

Poet T.S. Eliot's criticism of Kipling — "We expect to have to defend a poet against the charge of obscurity, we have to defend Kipling against the charge of excessive lucidity" — becomes a high compliment, a badge of honor, for legal writing. Few legal writers need to be defended against the charge of excessive lucidity. We should all aim and hope to be so indicted. Lucidity in legal writing is a good thing, something to be proud of.

THREE

THE PEN ORIGINATES THE THOUGHT

A close relationship exists between language and thought. Writing is a process of thought. It concentrates the mind. Nothing appears quite real until one has written about it. Writing is part of thinking.

"How do I know what I think," novelist E.M. Forster once said, "until I have written about it?" Or, as Montaigne supposedly said (according to Edgar Allan Poe): "People talk about thinking, but for my part I never think except when I sit down to write." By the same token, lawyers don't know what the argument really is until they write it.

In this sense, writing for lawyers is an adventure. We learn more about a case if we have to put our thoughts down on paper. It helps us think through a case or an argument. When you write it out yourself, you often learn things about the case that you hadn't realized before.

Producing a legal brief is therefore a process of searching. It means discovery: we discover what we want to argue in the process of writing. Each draft is experimental; the whole procedure is tentative.

An initial abstract idea or insight takes on more concreteness in the writing. The glimpse of an argument needs to be shaped, qualified, honed. It is what an artist does looking at a blank canvas and imagines a painting or a sculptor who sees a block of marble and imagines a statue. We too are artists of a sort. We look at the blank page with its infinite possibilities and, in the process of writing, sculpt an argument.

"When you go through the discipline of actually putting your argument in written form," Supreme Court Justice Samuel Alito explains, "you see problems with what you had thought out. When you are just thinking about a legal problem, your mind can easily skip over problems. When you have to write it, and if you aim for a tightly reasoned, well-expressed argument, very often that will expose the problems of the kind of argument that you had anticipated you were going to make."

The main excitement of the adventure comes in the writing. Writing creates thought. "How do I know what I mean 'till I see what I say?" Or, as Somerset Maugham, an underrated but wise writer, puts it in *The Summing Up*, "many writers think, not before, but as they write. The pen originates the thought.... The idea acquires substance by taking on a visible nature."

What a nice way of putting it: "The pen originates the thought."

FOUR

CLARITY

Putting ideas into writing is indispensable to clear thinking, and the heart of good legal writing is clarity. Once you learn how to make some silver writing bullets, you should know what you are trying to hit and aim at it. That is what we call clarity. Lack of clarity may not bother some philosophers and poets, but it does bother judges.

What really matters is making your meaning clear beyond a reasonable doubt. Above all other qualities, clarity is what you try to achieve. "The first quality, of course, that's necessary in writing is clarity," says Justice Alito, "so that you can understand what the lawyer is saying." If the key to real estate is "location, location, location," then the key to legal writing is clarity, clarity, clarity.

But "people often write obscurely," says Somerset Maugham, "because they have never taken the trouble to learn to write clearly."

Sometimes when you're having difficulty expressing something, it's because you really don't know exactly what you're trying to say. Maugham again: one "cause of obscurity is that the writer is himself not quite sure of his meaning. He has a vague impression of that he wants to say, but has not . . . formulated it in his mind and it is natural enough that he should not find a precise expression for a confused idea." Before starting any piece of legal writing, ask yourself: "Exactly what do I wish to say?" This question should provide clarity to the language you choose to use. Adds Alito, "there is a clear relationship between good, clear writing and good, clear thinking. And if you don't have one, it's very hard to have the other."

"The power of clear statement," declared Daniel Webster, "is the great power at the bar." Be sure that what you write accurately reflects what you think and what you mean to say. Mastery of language goes hand in hand with clarity of thought. Writing almost always clarifies what we are thinking. The act of writing forces us to be more precise.

Beware of abstractions. Legal writing is often about abstract concepts — like negligence, causation, duty — that generate hazy and vague verbal formulas that sound nice but are anything but clear and precise. Yet, "it is possible," in Maugham's words, "to express with lucidity the most subtle of reflections." In legal writing, generalities yield to concrete, detailed images. Ambiguity has its place in law as well as in poetry, but legal ambiguity is mainly for drafters of constitutions and great Supreme Court justices.

Until you become another Holmes or Cardozo — wonderful writers who sometimes sacrificed clarity to a memorable metaphor — you should aspire to clarity. Try to be direct, simple, brief, vigorous, and lucid. It is the first step in making yourself understood, and unless you make yourself understood you can't persuade a court, jury, adversary, or client to do what you want, which is the whole purpose of expressing yourself as a lawyer.

The consequences of foggy legal prose can be grave. Both the fog of law and the dangerous fog of war stem from not being able to see what is happening clearly. The dense fog surrounding the Court of Chancery in the opening chapter of Dickens's great novel *Bleak House* could also be an unforgettable image about legal writing.

FIVE

SOME SILVER BULLETS

Reading one little book will not alone make you a great legal writer, but at least it may help you to write better. It may make you more aware of things you can do every day to improve your legal writing. It may make you more self-conscious and aware of how you express yourself legally. To reach a high level of grace and style in legal writing takes daily practice, conscious effort, and real desire. It is worth the candle.

The goal of your legal writing is to persuade someone — client, adversary, judge or jury — to do something. Persuasion is the lawyer's Holy Grail. Malcolm Gladwell's comment (in the preface to *What the Dog Saw*) that "good writing does not succeed or fail on the strength of its ability to persuade" is untrue for legal writing, is the opposite of what good writing is for lawyers. Good legal writing largely depends on its ability to persuade. If it doesn't persuade, it has failed.

To achieve that goal, you have to write clearly, concisely, and cogently. You have to make your writing interesting. Here are some general suggestions, some silver bullets, many of which you may have heard before, some of them as far back as high school.

SILVER BULLET 5.1. Write. Write. Write. Up to now, what I have been saying has all been talk, and, even worse, airy talk about generalizations. You don't learn to write by talking; you learn to write by writing. You learn to do legal writing by writing legal papers. Write as many of them as you can. Push yourself to write more. Turn nothing down. Think of each project or assignment as a gift, a trip to the "legal writing gym," an opportunity to flex and exercise your legal writing muscles, and develop some writing muscle memory.

"You cannot write well," our friend Maugham says in *The Summing Up*, "unless you write much, unless you form a habit."

SILVER BULLET 5.2. Getting better takes time. The mysterious thing we call talent, or genius, does not spring to life full-fledged — at least not in lawyer brief-writers. Instead it becomes apparent at the end of many long years of discipline and perseverance. No brief-writing prodigies exist.

Great skill in many fields requires thousands of hours of practice. So too with legal writing. Skill at legal writing also takes much practice. Good legal writers build their skills gradually over the course of their careers, improving their work slowly over long periods.

SILVER BULLET 5.3. Start writing as soon as possible. Don't wait until you have finished all possible research. Write first, research later. Usually you have an idea or a general sense of what the main points of your argument are. Based on that, make a tentative outline and start putting your thoughts together. Analyze the problem or develop the argument on paper *before* exhaustive research. Legal research can often be, or at least seem to be, never ending. Get a draft done early on.

Literary excellence is in the revisions. Delaying actual writing may cause writer's block or leave insufficient time for revising. Start writing no matter what. The water does not flow until the faucet is turned on. And remember what Maugham says about the pen (or computer) originating the thought, and the idea acquiring substance by becoming visible on paper.

SILVER BULLET 5.4. Don't write like a lawyer, avoid legalese. Write as a person unspoiled by the law. Write conversationally. Use plain English. Don't try to show off by sounding like a lawyer. Avoid legalisms; avoid Latin phrases (*e.g.*, arguendo, inter alia); avoid legal jargon (*e.g.*, "the above-captioned matter," "the undersigned," "the instant case," "thereof," "therein," "herein," "said," "hereinafter").

For example, "the above-captioned matter," "the above-referenced matter," "the instant case" can all easily be replaced by much shorter and simpler "this case." Write to be understood.

Some examples:

Better	Legalese
despite, in spite of, even though	notwithstanding
explain	elucidate
show	evince
guess	hypothesize
among other things	inter alia
for the sake of argument	arguendo
before	prior to
after, later	subsequent to, subsequently
about	approximately
under	pursuant to
this case	the above-referenced matter, the instant case, the case at bar,
clear	beyond peradventure

This rule adapts to legal writing the following rule from George Orwell's classic essay "Politics and the English Language": "Never use a foreign phrase, a scientific word or a jargon word if you can think of an everyday English equivalent."

SILVER BULLET 5.5. Always be aware of your audience. Look at the issues through the eyes of your readers. Consider how your target will respond to what you are writing. Think about the judge's background, his or her prior rulings, what part of the country you are in, the local customs and mores.

SILVER BULLET 5.6. Speak what you write; hear how it sounds. Make your sentences pleasing to the ear as well as to the eye. "One aims at rhythm and balance," says novelist Maugham. "One reads a sentence aloud to see [hear?] if it sounds well." "Some things strike my ear differently," says Chief Justice Roberts, "and that's very important. And I'll spend a lot of time trying to get a sentence to read in a way that seems comfortable and well paced and conveys the meaning and isn't choppy." Too little attention is paid by most writers to sound, and too many writers are tone deaf.

Good writers test the rightness of their words out loud, the impact of words on the ear, the music of language. They know it's all about the music of the speech, more than the logic or the substance. Good prose, when read aloud, reveals different rhythms and tunes and stays in the mind for that reason. Really well-written prose tends to be composed in a musical fashion that depends on rhythm.

Think of Martin Luther King's "I Have A Dream" speech, Churchill's World War II speeches, Lincoln's Gettysburg Address, and JFK's Inaugural Address. Rhetorically sensitive writing can, to some extent, create a ready reception and response to the message by the way in which the sentences are crafted. Try to develop a good ear for how language sounds (as well as a good eye for how it appears on the page), an ability to LISTEN to what you are attempting to do.

According to biographer Carl Sandburg, as Lincoln "would finish a sentence or a paragraph he read it out loud usually to see how it would sound; the sound of the words helped him to see more clearly what he was saying."

Memorable legal phrasing is the same. "Danger invites rescue" is one of Cardozo's most permanent sentences because it stays in the mind due to its sound. Three words, each of two syllables, register powerfully on the mind's ear.

The brief-writer who can appreciate the power of language might also become a compelling oral advocate.

SILVER BULLET 5.7. Avoid Wordiness. Be concise. Prolixity is a common complaint about legal writing. Streamline your writing. This advice is particularly important in an age of page limits. "If I said more," Dorothea Brooke says in George Eliot's *Middlemarch*, "it would only be the same thing written out at greater length."

Pare unnecessary words. Or, in Orwell's rule, "If it is possible to cut a word out, always cut it out." You will be surprised how often you can trim by cutting words.

SILVER BULLET 5.8. Prefer short words to long ones, and short sentences to long ones. Or, again as George Orwell put it: "Never use a long word where a short one will do." In 1903, Justice Holmes advised his young friend Lewis Einstein to "diminish somewhat your use of words of Latin derivation. A sentence gets its force from short words." And in 1897, a young Winston Churchill wrote an essay called "Scaffolding of Rhetoric," in which he said, "Audiences prefer short homely words of common usage. The shorter words of common usage. The shorter words of a language are usually the more ancient. Their meaning is more ingrained in the national character and they appeal with greater force to simple understanding than words recently introduced from the Latin and the Greek."

You're not Proust or Henry James. Keep your sentences short. Gustave Flaubert, who knew something about writing, put it deftly and memorably: "whenever you can shorten a sentence, do. And one always can. The best sentence? The shortest." *Cf.* Rudolf Flesch, *The Art of Readable Writing* (1949) (a somewhat overly simplistic book, but good on short sentences enhancing reading comprehension).

But bear in mind that in some cases a short word simply will not do. Big words can help to highlight well-chosen short ones. A good example is: "The life of the law has not been logic, it has been experience." Perhaps the most famous sentence in American law, it mostly uses short, ordinary, easily comprehended words.

Of the thirteen words in Holmes's sentence, all but two are small, common words of one syllable. And the two words that have more than one syllable are distinguished that way for a reason. Those two words — "logic" and "experience" — are set off for purposes of special emphasis. Both of them are simple yet absolutely key to the sense of the passage. Their increased number of syllables draws attention to them for greater effect. None of the words is jargon. Anyone can read the sentence and understand it.

Of course, style is much more than words alone, whether long or short. **SILVER BULLET 5.9. Keep paragraphs relatively short and tight**. A paragraph should generally be no more than four or five sentences. Give the reader a break. A paragraph that covers a whole page is daunting. I've seen paragraphs in briefs that go on for two or more pages. And remember that the occasional one-sentence paragraph can be effective and get attention.

"I have no desire to read a book without paragraph breaks," writer Elisa Gabbert says in *The Word Pretty*. "A lack of white space on the page makes me feel a little panicky, like being on a train in an underground tunnel — where's my exit strategy?"

SILVER BULLET 5.10. Use many headings and subheadings.

Think visually. Little pieces are easier to read. Headings can be used very effectively to highlight the key topics, emphasize the main points, and break up long sections of text. Even if the reader only skims the brief, if the headings are crisp and summarize the main points, the facts and the arguments will come through. Try to have at least one heading or subheading on each page. A whole page of type without any heading breaks is intimidating and off-putting.

SILVER BULLET 5.11. Deploy strong topic sentences. A reader should have to use little effort to follow your writing. Topic sentences are important, helpful road signs to the reader. Busy people — such as judges, their law clerks, and lawyers — often skim read by looking at only the first sentence of paragraphs. (I, for one, do this. You probably do, too.) That means topic sentences take on even more significance.

SILVER BULLET 5.12. Remember the stress points. A topic sentence is a stress point. The key points in any component of writing are the beginning and end. The first and last word of a sentence, the first and last sentence of a paragraph — these are what your reader will remember. Use that knowledge. Don't bury your "lede," as journalists say.

If you put the main point, the upshot of your paragraph, in the last sentence, it could get lost, especially if the reader is skimming. In that case, repeat that key last sentence in slightly revised form as the topic sentence of the next paragraph. That way, it won't be lost or overlooked.

SILVER BULLET 5.13. Vary your sentence structure and length. A brief composed of all short sentences one after the other would be choppy and a chore to read. Change the length of sentences. Make many of them simple, declarative sentences, make others more complex. Use sentence structure to highlight your main point.

SILVER BULLET 5.14. Favor strong nouns and verbs over adjectives and adverbs. "I am more suspicious of adjectives," wrote Carl Sandburg at the age of 89, "than at any other time in all my born days."

SILVER BULLET 5.15. Use action verbs and the active voice. "The rule applies here" is better than "The rule is applicable here." "To be" verbs such as "is" and "are" sound weak. So too with the passive voice. "The court ruled...." is better that "It was ruled by the court that...."

SILVER BULLET 5.16. Smooth Transitions. Your readers need roadmaps for your writing. Transitions signal the reader, they tell the reader where you are going, and that is important. But, for some reason, many lawyers think they have to use crutch transition words at the start of every paragraph. Those crutch words take form of numbering (first, second, third. . . .) or "however," "although," "moreover," furthermore," "for example," "next," "finally," and the like. These are elementary forms of transition that often can be eliminated or improved for smoothness and style and subtle elegance.

On the other hand (transition), some transitions work better at the beginning of a sentence. For example, starting a sentence with "And" or "In addition" signals to the reader you are coming up with another reason for the same point. Likewise, "But" at the beginning of a sentence tells the reader you are showing the other side.

The classiest and most subtle transition is by idea. Let the idea of one paragraph or point lead naturally and logically into the next paragraph or point. Frequently the last sentence of a paragraph will contain a key word that can be repeated in the first sentence of the next paragraph and thereby supply all the transition you need without an obvious crutch word.

If the transition signal words must be used, they often make for easier reading if not put in the beginning of a sentence but in the middle. "However," "moreover," "furthermore," "for example," go better in the middle of a sentence. It is frequently smoother that way.

SILVER BULLET 5.17. Avoid modifier words. We all tend to use words that we think stress the point we are trying to make, but really don't. Words such as the following add nothing: very, quite, rather, somewhat, really, in fact, just, so, pretty, of course, surely, that said, apparently. Try not to use them.

SILVER BULLET 5.18. Avoid false emphatics. We lawyers also like to use words such as: certainly, clearly, obviously, undoubtedly, manifestly, plainly, clear beyond peradventure, egregious, totally inapposite. We think such words emphasize how right we are. Not so.

Such words are red flags that add nothing to meaning and beg to be proven wrong. They invite rebuttal and refutation, which can be embarrassing. We (judges especially) see the introductory word "clearly" (or a similar word), and we think some doubtful thing follows, usually the most doubtful thing in issue. Demonstrate you are "clearly" correct by marshaling your arguments, your authorities, your facts. Let them speak for you and show how you are "obviously" right, without relying on words that dare the reader to prove false.

SILVER BULLET 5.19. Avoid self-reflexive phrases. Lawyers often put such phrases like "as discussed (demonstrated) (shown) (above) (below)" at the beginning of sentences, and thereby weaken the force of whatever comes next. Just say what you want to say. If you feel the need, add a cite at the end of the sentence. Exs: "___. *See* Point III below; see above at 3."

SILVER BULLET 5.20. Avoid wasteful, useless, tentative, throat-clearing lead-ins. Many lawyers write meaningless verbose, unnecessary things like: "We think...," "we believe...," "in our opinion," "we submit...," "it is interesting to note that...," "needless to say...," "it goes without saying," "it is to be noted that...," "at this point in time," "at the end of the day," "in the final analysis," "the fact of the matter is," "it is submitted that," "as a matter of fact," "it is well settled that," "it is clear that," "it should not be forgotten that," "it should be remembered that," or "the Court is undoubtedly well aware of...."

Just say whatever it is you have to say without the time-wasting run-up. If something is "needless to say" or "goes without saying," then don't say it.

SILVER BULLET 5.21. Avoid unnecessary, courtier-like phrases such as "we respectfully request that...." You are not a flunky in the court of Louis XIV, who has to scrape, bow and kowtow at every opportunity. And judges are not royalty. We are all members of the same profession, each with our appropriate roles, and the people we call judges happen to be in temporary, brief authority. Using "respectfully" other than in signing a brief as "respectfully submitted" or signing off a letter to a judge "respectfully yours" strikes me as awkward and overmuch servility and reverence bordering on flummery.

SILVER BULLET 5.22. Avoid hyperbole, sarcasm, and personality attacks. In our desire to represent clients zealously, we can sometimes forget how we appear to those reading what we write. Do not make inflammatory personal attacks on opposing counsel or the judge. Such attacks are unprofessional, alienate the reader, and are strategically unwise and may backfire. "You should aim to persuade the judge," advises Justice Ginsburg, "by the power of *your* reasoning and not by denigrating the other side."

SILVER BULLET 5.23. Avoid words that reduce your credibility. Similarly, it does not help your case to call your opponent's position or the lower court judge's decision, things like "ridiculous," "absurd," "nonsense," "disingenuous," "a joke," or "preposterous." "Self-serving" is another phrase to steer clear of. Since all helpful evidence or testimony is by definition "self-serving," it is not a proper evidentiary objection in court and is not a proper criticism of an adversary's presentation. Those words are no more than many adjectives and amount to mere name-calling. They are not argument or demonstration, and prove nothing. Show, don't tell. Let readers come to the conclusions you want after you show why they should. By avoiding such adjectives, you command credibility.

SILVER BULLET 5.24. Repetition is a two-edged sword. A theory in salesmanship says that if the virtues of a product are repeated over and over again, people eventually start to believe them, no matter how unreal those virtues are. Propaganda proceeds on the same premise. Many lawyers subscribe to this theory and repeat the same points, in almost identical language, again and again in a brief. But be careful. Repetition does not transform a lie into a truth. But....

SILVER BULLET 5.25. Beliefs vs. Facts. Remember, as Daniel Kahneman has explained, the "emotional tail wags the rational dog." Building a relationship in which you instill in the judge an awareness and willingness to view the evidence and the law in the case through the lens you offer starts with an understanding that feelings come first, even with judges. They read your brief with a wealth of personal experiences that affect how they view issues and how they have resolved cases in the past. What they think, what they feel and how they make decisions have evolved over the course of their professional lives. You should take account of these biases, preloads, predispositions, tendencies and partialities. Recognize the power of the first impression and initial feelings and how they must be managed. Figure out how to engage and motivate the judge. Read Daniel Kahneman's *Thinking Fast and Slow*.

Recent years have once again underscored that truth is often not persuasive, because beliefs and emotions can be impervious to facts. Rational argument makes little or no headway against emotion or faith. Think of any argument you ever had about religion or love or politics. Beliefs always outweigh facts, which allows some people to cry "fake news" and gives rise to "alternative facts." That is the human condition. Just consider how little effect "facts" had on the question of President Trump's impeachment. People's minds were set, one way or the other, regardless of facts.

You have to know, respect, and find common ground with your audience, and take their feelings into account. Those feelings could be much more appealing than reason and fact.

An audience's receptivity to facts depends on its feelings and impulses and sensibility. A "fact" is not a mere intellectual conception; to be accepted, it needs a dynamic power to move individuals and drive them to believe and accept it. Facts are more easily accepted if they are consistent with the thought and prevailing conception of life and values.

SILVER BULLET 5.26. Avoid clichés and platitudes. This is obvious, but "easier said than done," to use a cliché. We often think in terms of clichés because we hear and read them so frequently, and they usually contain a germ of truth. The first time they were used, it was nice and vivid, but now they are old and tired. A common example in legal writing is the trite phrase: such and such a major case "and its progeny." Thoughtlessly used, as in "Roe v. Wade and its progeny," the cliché can awkwardly misfire as the leading case on the constitutional right to abortion is described as having descendants. The mind does a double take. Try as best you can to root trite phrases out of your writing. Orwell: "Never use a metaphor, simile or other figure of speech which you are used to seeing in print."

SILVER BULLET 5.27. Use demonstrative evidence in your writing. Persuasion takes many forms. People absorb and retain information in many ways. Reading is only one of the ways. A visual presentation of some kind may illustrate, clarify, reinforce, or emphasize a point or argument better than mere words, no matter how well expressed. Charts and graphs can be more effective than text. Examples: charts, diagrams, graphs, pictures, tables, models, poster boards, skeletons, and other visual aids all supplement and the leave a deeper impression than the written word alone.

SILVER BULLET 5.28. Names. Three related rules apply here. (1) After the first time you mention a party (*e.g.*, Plaintiff John Jones), just call him or her by their last name rather than plaintiff, defendant, appellant, respondent, and so on. It avoids confusion.

(2) Once a person – party or otherwise – is introduced with both first and last name, thereafter just use their last name without Mr., Ms., or whatever. While Mr. and Ms. may seem polite, it is simply clutter.

(3) Except for familiar ones (*e.g.*, SEC, NAACP, UN), avoid acronyms and initials for names, a common habit for lawyers. Seeing lots of letters in an unfamiliar format does not help comprehension or identification.

SILVER BULLET 5.29. Be wary of footnotes. Judges (and their clerks) are busy people with too much to read. They are likely to skip footnotes in briefs, which burden the text with numbers. Some appellate courts will not consider arguments in footnotes. So avoid substantive footnotes.

Fred Rodell called footnotes "phony excrescences," and Judge Abner Mikva, in a 1985 article entitled "Goodbye to Footnotes," labeled them an "abomination." They also distract and interrupt.*Some courts actually forbid footnotes in briefs. Check local rules. Footnotes are, however, excellent homes for string cites.

"There's no point using a footnote," Justice Arthur Goldberg once said. "If you want to put something in a footnote, make a decision: Is it relevant and important or not? If it's important to your argument, put it in the text. And if it's not important, throw it out."

But opinion is not unanimous about footnotes. They are the subjects of lively debate. Judge Edward R. Becker wrote a 1996 law review article "In Praise of Footnotes." Many good lawyers (and judges) put substantive points in footnotes. So you have to use your judgment. I favor no, or only a few, footnotes. A lone footnote in a twenty-page brief can actually be an eye-catching way to stress a point.

Bryan Garner, a leading commentator on legal writing, favors putting all citations into footnotes so as not to slow down the flow of the argument in the text. Following Garner's advice makes a brief look odd, and the reader's eye has to constantly go to the bottom of the page. I have tried the Garner approach and did not like it. Garner's is a small minority anyway.

---

* (This is the only footnote in this book.) Remember what Noel Coward famously said: "Having to read footnotes resembles having to go downstairs to answer the door while in the midst of making love." For a contrary view from a cultural historian and scholar, *see* Gertrude Himmelfarb, "Where Have All the Footnotes Gone?" in her *On Looking into the Abyss* (1994).

Many briefs have an early footnote explaining citations to the record. Most of the time such a footnote is unnecessary because the record references in the text are perfectly clear. Consider using this kind of footnote only where textual references are ambiguous or confusing.

SILVER BULLET 5.30. Avoid "there is" and "there are." These are weak constructions and miss the opportunity for stress at the start of a sentence. Compare "There are many cases that support out position" with "Many cases support our position." Which is the stronger phrasing?

SILVER BULLET 5.31. The secret to writing well is to rewrite and rewrite. Truman Capote said that, "good writing is rewriting." And according to John McPhee, perhaps America's best living non-fiction writer: "the essence of the process is revision." The same applies to legal writing. Copyedit your writing.

SILVER BULLET 5.32. Proofread, and then proofread again, for all the obvious reasons. You don't want a judge, your adversary, your client, or your senior partner to find typos, misspellings, or any other mistakes. Sweat the small stuff.

SILVER BULLET 5.33. Surprise your reader. Legal writing need not be dull. Make your writing interesting. A lot of reading competes for our attention. We all have too much to read. A judge or client or another lawyer might have to read your writing, but he or she does not have to like it. You have to make them like it. Make your point vivid so people pay attention and don't zone out.

The easiest decision a reader can make is to stop reading. This means that every sentence has to count in grabbing and holding the reader's attention, starting with the first. Get to the point.

* * *

Any set of rules has to be interpreted and applied with common sense, wisdom, and judgment. You could follow all of them and still produce bad legal writing. "Break any of these rules sooner than say anything outright barbaric," is the way Orwell put it after his own list of writing rules. These suggestions will take on more meaning in concrete contexts.

SIX

BRIEFS AND LEGAL MEMORANDA

For those of you who like expository writing (and most of us lawyers do), briefs and legal memos are where you get to strut your stuff. For most litigators, brief-writing is the best part of legal writing, at once the most fun and the most demanding. Approach it with joy and anticipation. The prospect of writing a legal brief should stir your blood, and you should rise to it like a lion lifting up at the smell of impala. It should be instinctual, incurable, unanswerable, and a calling, not a choice.

Writing a brief is a many-sided, golden opportunity for creative lawyering. It is a blank canvas waiting for the lawyer's artistic touch. "Unfortunately," according to Justice Ginsburg, "many lawyers don't appreciate the importance of how one expresses oneself . . . most importantly in brief-writing."

A brief is a piece of written advocacy that cries out for imagination. But most books about brief-writing dwell on the mechanics of that task, without mentioning, much less stressing, creativity. Bryan Garner's book *The Winning Brief* is a rare exception.

"Few legal writers," Garner points out, "seem to think of their work as being essentially creative. They often think that writing well is simply a matter of finding the law and getting it down." On the contrary, Garner correctly says, "every brief presents opportunities for creativity — for imaginative approaches." Absolutely. We can try to make our legal briefs into at least minor works of art.

In setting forth the facts, for instance, the lawyer becomes a short story writer who can sequence, describe, and stress those facts in a way most favorable to the client.

Similarly, the points of argument can be creatively ordered to make the greatest impact. Narrative and analysis obviously draw on creativity. But there is more.

We are tempted to say, in a paraphrase of Tolstoy's opening of *Anna Karenina*, that good legal briefs are all alike, and every bad legal brief is bad in its own way.

In general keep your briefs as short as possible. Bear in mind Samuel Johnson's famous reaction to Milton's epic poem "Paradise Lost": "None ever wish it longer. Its perusal is a duty rather than a pleasure." Sounding like Dr. Johnson, Chief Justice Roberts has said, "I have yet to put down a brief and say, 'I wish that had been longer,' . . . Almost every brief I've read could be shorter." After all, the key word is "brief."

You don't have to use all the pages you are allowed to use. Keep your arguments direct and concise. Be accurate and intellectually honest in your arguments. Keep your prose calm and clear. Do not make jokes. Avoid sarcasm and insults. Avoid extraneous information.

Make your brief a lucid, simple, non-repetitive presentation. Writing a brief requires a clear thesis, backed by rigorously marshaled evidence, in the service of a persuasive argument. The judge needs to understand how you are thinking about the case and why your client should prevail. The judge cannot understand these things unless your writing guides the judge's thinking.

Don't overcomplicate the writing or the message. Simplicity is power. Sweat blood over it. If dates, places, and names of people are not helpful or relevant to understand the argument or the ruling, omit them. Include only crucial details. To avoid confusion, use the parties' names rather than plaintiff, defendant, appellant, or respondent.

SILVER BULLET 6.1. Weaponize Preliminary Statements

Every brief starts from the same point: the opening line and the first few sentences that follow, what journalists call the "lede." Make them count. They can be ponderous and downright dull. Or they can grab you by the lapels, pull you close and into your world immediately and scream in your face: "read this."

The first paragraph, especially the first sentence, of a brief should be as attention-getting as any other lede in a piece of writing. You want a great opening line, your own version of "Call me Ishmael," or "It is a truth universally acknowledged, that a single man in possession of a good fortune must be in want of a wife," or "It was the best of times, it was the worst of times."

You want to draw readers in, hold their interest, and make them keep on reading. You want the beginning to be riveting, compelling, as you set the stage for your arguments in a clear and concise manner. You want to be creative, to promote your argument and show that you have some style. You want to create the tone and compel the reader to go on. You want to write so that the reader does not lose interest along the way.

The introduction is key. It should distill the essence of the case, it should contain the conclusion. Avoid the boring, tiresome, ridiculously uninformative opening line used habitually by far too many brief writers: "This brief is submitted by (plaintiff)(defendant) in support of (in opposition to) the motion for...." Such an opening sentence is worse than trite, it is a missed opportunity.

It is plagued by flaws. It is dull, commonplace, mechanical, formulaic. It is repetitive, for the title of the brief, right above the preliminary statement, says it all: "PLAINTIFF'S BRIEF IN SUPPORT OF SUMMARY JUDGMENT." Why say the same thing again in the very first sentence, and lose the wonderful opportunity to craft a catchy lede?

With a little bit of imagination and effort, we can always do better, much better. Be creative. Many briefs easily give rise to interesting, fun, opening sentences and opening paragraphs. The first sentence of a brief, like a newspaper lede, is a wonderful opportunity to grab a reader's interest and start to persuade. Crisp, cogent ledes are as useful for lawyers as they are for journalists. The lede is a signpost, a means of orienting the reader to the path to be taken, a way to tell the reader how to make sense of what follows.

The argument starts with the first sentence, which is a stress point, a point of emphasis. We should come up with, that is, create, our own effective and memorable first line. How about the following opening lines taken from actual briefs:

1. "The long-delayed opposing papers from plaintiff were hardly worth the wait."

2. "Plaintiff's opposition papers illustrate the law of unintended consequences. Rather than demonstrating why dismissal should be denied, plaintiff's opposing brief actually shows why his amended complaint should be dismissed."

3. This is a meritless case, brought in the wrong court, based on an imaginary, implausible, unsubstantiated, unenforceable oral contract."

4. "There are times when a plaintiff who brings a baseless lawsuit and causes blameless defendants to incur substantial legal fees should not be allowed to preserve its option and escape any consequences simply by filing a voluntary notice of discontinuance. This is one of those times."

5. "With this appeal, appellants persist in their ill-conceived attempt to enforce a non-existent, superseded non-compete clause."

6. "This case is about an attorney-client relationship that soured in the brine of lawyer overreaching and deception."

7. "Sometimes a lawyer's brief inadvertently or subconsciously reveals much more than the author intended. When that happens, we occasionally see into the heart of the matter. That insight is exactly what has now occurred with plaintiff's brief."

8. "This is a case about fairness and common sense as against an arbitrary rule."

9. "Cardozo's words — 'What a cobweb of five-spun casuistry'! — fit the opposition's brief perfectly."

10. "In a free society, people's livelihoods should not depend on their holding 'correct' political views, as defined by their government or their employer."

11. "Plaintiff continues his intentional forum-shopping spree."

12. "Respondent's brief understandably runs away from the stipulation at issue."

13. "This is a motion to prevent grossly disproportional — and therefore unconstitutional — penalties in a First Amendment context from taking effect before being scrutinized by this Court. The purpose is to preserve the status quo for judicial review."

14. "This arbitration arises from Respondents' corporate raiding of the bond department of Claimant, which forced Claimant to close the department and incur millions of dollars in losses."

15. "This appeal arises from the lower court's fundamental misapprehension of the obligations a publisher owed to its author."

16. "The overarching question raised by this appeal is whether the requirements for pleading securities fraud related to the on-going financial crisis should be applied in a way that ensures the accountability of corporate executives or in a way that shelters executives from being judged for their conduct. To pose the question is to answer it, and the answer explains why the decision below dismissing appellants' securities fraud action should be reversed."

17. "To avoid their obligation as non-party witnesses to produce vital evidence, respondents wrap themselves in the First Amendment. It is a poor fit."

18. "This is a strike suit masquerading as a trademark dispute."

19. "The time has come to bring down the curtain on this farce." [Case about the disputed funding of a Broadway show].

20. "Plaintiff's answering papers are like this winter's weather. Having experienced several snowstorms this season, we and the Court know a blizzard when we see one. Plaintiff's opposition is a blizzard of irrelevancies designed to blind the Court. But this winter has taught us all how to deal effectively with all sorts of blizzards, this one included."

21. "Every so often a complaint is filed that has so many fatal flaws and defects, is barred at the threshold by so many legal doctrines, that a lawyer almost does not know where to start in structuring a motion to dismiss. The abundance of defenses almost bewilders the conscientious brief-writer. This is such a case. The amended complaint is a law professor's dream. It reads like a bizarre hypothetical on a civil procedure examination testing a first-year student's ability to spot all the several reasons why a pleading should be thrown out. . . . When a complaint is so riddled with fundamental error, it should be dismissed at the outset."

22. "This is a 'perfect storm' of an appeal. It combines international terrorism, free speech, the Internet, and something called 'libel tourism.' Fused into one appeal, these various elements come to this Court from federal court filtered through a certified question of long-arm jurisdiction.

"Law responds to new developments, what Holmes famously called 'the felt necessities of the time.' A new development in our time is libel tourism. This appeal asks the Court to help mitigate the pernicious effects of libel tourism by finding personal jurisdiction over a foreign serial libel tourist who has obtained a libel judgment in England against a New York author. Threatened enforcement of that judgment has had a chilling effect in New York on that author and others.

"The certified question gives the Court an opportunity to protect the rights of plaintiff and other New York residents to write about — and all New Yorkers to read about — urgent public issues such as the financing of international terrorism. A finding of personal jurisdiction over this defendant will enable New York authors and publishers to obtain effective relief from foreign libel judgments designed to target and restrict their speech in New York."

23. "The cross-motions for summary judgment in this diversity action require the Court to interpret a 'libel and allied torts' insurance policy in the publishing field. The Court's interpretation will have far-ranging effects."

24. "Clausewitz famously said 'war is the continuation of politics by other means.' In a disturbing but unmistakable twist on Clausewitz, [defendant's] opposing brief treats litigation as the continuation of contract negotiation by other means."

* * *

Each one of these real-life openings from briefs draws the reader in and starts to persuade from the get-go. They are interesting, even fun to read. It is not simply a matter of your writing skill; it is a matter of the spirit, the attitude in which you approach your task. Why be a slave to the way others write?

We need not blindly imitate or lazily perpetuate bad practices, no matter how old or widespread. You have a good, independent mind that can draw on all your education, ability, professional experience, reading and knowledge of the world and of human beings to *create* an effective, original opening line for *your* brief that persuades the court to see the world as your client sees it. With a bit of imagination, most legal briefs can begin memorably.

Either in the Preliminary Statement or right after it, try to summarize, in a few paragraphs or lines, why the court should grant the relief you are seeking. Think of it as an executive summary of the arguments to come, often it is labeled "Summary of the Argument." These introductory paragraphs should convey as much possible as succinctly as possible, identifying the major points and providing both an overview of and a road map for the arguments to come. I often have a short, punchy section entitled: "Why the Motion Should Be Granted (or Denied)," which includes bullet points that aid and focus the reader's attention. A good rule of thumb is to assume that judges and their law clerks only read the first four pages of your brief or memorandum of law. Get all you absolutely need to say in these first four pages.

As a practical matter, write the Preliminary Statement or Introduction last. It only takes shape in your mind after you have thought through and written everything else. That way, you have a better sense of the whole and a firmer grasp of the true essence and thrust of the overall argument. You will then have an easier time writing the beginning.

The basic idea is to start with something that grabs the attention of the judge so the judge wants to read more. Then create a summary for the judge, followed by a concise structure that is easy to grasp.

SILVER BULLET 6.2. Describe the Procedural Posture

The procedural posture of a case is a vital piece of information for the reader of a brief and situates the relief requested. Tell the reader as soon as possible whether we are dealing with a pre-trial or post-trial motion, a motion for summary judgment or to dismiss, a discovery motion. This information makes a difference. Also reveal if a prior ruling affects the current request.

Without such information up front, the brief can look like a disembodied collection of facts without an anchor. But setting forth the procedural posture of a case does not mean you have to recite everything that happened since the complaint was filed. Include only what is relevant.

SILVER BULLET 6.3. Set Forth the Applicable Legal Standard

It helps to have a short section just before the Argument that sets forth the legal standards governing the requested relief, including the standard of review on an appeal. Such a section provides everyone with a framework, and a target if someone disagrees. Is the standard "abuse of discretion" or "de novo" review?

But be sensible. The legal standards for some issues are so well known and familiar that one need not waste precious brief space in repeating them. To set forth at length the standards for summary judgment or motions to dismiss, for example, is unproductive. Judges can recite those standards in their sleep; they don't need to be reminded of them. Of course, if there is some special wrinkle that controls your case, that is a different story. But it is unnecessary to explain for pages that disputed issues of fact require denial of summary judgment. Just show, in the argument, that disputed issues of material fact exist.

SILVER BULLET 6.4. State the Facts Effectively

Here is where you often win or lose. Spend time on the Statement of Facts. Every lawsuit is a story, every case has a good theme, find it, identify it, and use the statement of facts to demonstrate it and bring it to life. Lawyers, as well as novelists, must be skillful narrative crafters, pruning and stretching the unruly features of real life to awaken and maintain interest and sympathy. Use chronology for the narrative. Try to tell a good, compelling story of injustice.

Stories are how people process information. Use a time sequence rather than a witness-by-witness account unless you are purposely attempting to create a Rashomon-like description. Maybe even include a fact that may not bear directly on the issue, but livens the presentation and adds a little human interest.

Also, rather than calling it the neutral "statement of facts," try to label it something more argumentative or persuasive.

SILVER BULLET 6.5. Make the Argument Logical and Clear

Your argument should be a persuasive presentation of why you are right. Spend as much time as possible on organizing and structuring the argument. Use an outline, and modify that outline as you go along. Usually, but not always, the argument requires a logical development. You want the court to see, understand, and share the steps of your reasoning. To do this, it is essential to make an outline and to think in terms of basic logic.

One good approach is to rely, in effect, on a syllogism. Recall from your college philosophy or logic course the familiar example of the syllogism:

> Major Premise: All men are mortal.
> Minor Premise: Socrates is a man
> Conclusion: Socrates is mortal.

The syllogism easily lends itself to legal argument. For instance:

Major Premise:	The statute of limitation says a suit for libel mustbe filed within one year of publication
Minor Premise:	The plaintiff filed his libel suit more than one year after publication
Conclusion:	The libel suit is barred by the statute of limitation

Any number of fact patterns can follow the syllogism form of argument effectively.

Another excellent approach is to think of your argument as resembling the type of proof you used in high school geometry class. A geometric proof involves writing reasoned, logical explanations that use definitions, axioms, postulates, and previously proved theorems to arrive at a conclusion about a geometric statement. In essence, it is an argument that begins with known facts, proceeds from there through a series of logical deductions, and ends with the point you are trying to prove. You have to spell out every little step in your reasoning so your argument doesn't have any gaps.

As applied to law, this means regarding your legal conclusion as the hypothesis or "To Prove" statement. Then you proceed to list each step in your argument and explain why we know it is true. Using this chain or reasoning you can often see for yourself what must be shown to convince the reader you are right in your legal conclusion. It frequently helps to chart, diagram or outline the steps in your argument.

Think hard about your argument. Use your facts as best you can. Beyond simple analysis of case precedent, broaden your argument in terms of fairness, history and policy considerations. Choose one case, with facts as similar as possible, to discuss at some length; deal with other cases with brief description, perhaps in parentheticals — a judge should not have to look up a case to know why you have cited it. Avoid string cites. If you must use them for some reason, put them in footnotes.

SILVER BULLET 6.6. Use the Most Effective Sequence of Points

Focus on your best arguments, rather than a blunderbuss, scattershot approach. Quickly and often present your theme. Organize your presentation in terms of persuasiveness, not logic. Put your best argument first, even if it is not logical to do so. In other words, don't start with a jurisdictional argument unless it is your best argument or unless a court rule requires it. To start with a weak jurisdictional argument, while perhaps logical, is not the right way to persuade a court.

SILVER BULLET 6.7. Write Persuasive Point Headings

Many lawyers treat point headings in a brief as if they were vague subject markers in an outline rather than steps in an argument in a brief. Compare:

Just Okay	Better
I	I
THE COMPLAINT DOES NOT STATE A CAUSE OF ACTION	SINCE PLAINTIFF DOES NOT ALLEGE PERFORMANCE, NOR ANY EXCUSE FOR NON-PERFORMANCE, HE CANNOT RECOVER FOR BREACH OF CONTRACT
II	II
NO CONTRACT CAME INTO BEING	SINCE DEFENDANT'S CIRCULAR DID NOT STATE ANY TERMS CONCERNING THE QUANTITY OR PRICE OF GOODS ADVERTISED, IT WAS NOT AN OFFER THAT COULD HAVE BEEN ACCEPTED
III	III
PLAINTIFF IS BARRED BY THE STATUTE OF LIMITATIONS	SINCE PLAINTIFF DELAYED THREE YEARS BEFORE SUING FOR LIBEL, THE SUIT IS BARRED BY THE APPLICABLE ONE-YEAR STATUTE OF LIMITATIONS

The point heading should be a concise argumentative statement applying a specific principle to the facts of the particular case. It should be a clear and complete statement forcefully written. It should not be a statement of an abstract principle of law. It should be interesting and informative.

Opinion is split on this issue. Many good lawyers prefer the simple, declarative point head, such as those on the left above. I think such a heading resembles a placeholder in an outline rather than a compelling step in an argument that moves the reader along. The best advice I can give is for you to try it both ways and see which way you like better.

SILVER BULLET 6.8. Use Quotations Carefully

Quote judiciously from authorities, courts or others. Avoid long quotations and use block quotes rarely. The eye tends to skip over them. Paraphrase and quote the best nuggets.

SILVER BULLET 6.9. Tell a Court What It "Should" Do, Not What It "Must" Do

Be sensitive to how you argue. Care about tone. Judges, like everyone else, do not appreciate being told they "must" do something. Regardless of how right you are on the merits, resist the temptation to instruct a court what it "must" do. "Should" is less confrontational and goes over better. Say "the Court should dismiss the action" rather than "the Court must dismiss the action." Be aware of your audience and its psychology.

SILVER BULLET 6.10. Regain the Offensive: Avoid Counterproductive Formulaic Style in Answering Opposing Arguments

An opportunity for creative brief writing arises when composing a section of your brief that answers an argument of your adversary. But that opportunity is frequently overlooked.

It is common in legal briefs, especially a brief in opposition, for lawyers to set up their arguments by paraphrasing their opponents' arguments in the topic sentence of a section of a brief. Many brief writers will start important sections of their briefs with topic sentences such as "Plaintiff [or defendant] argues that" and proceed to restate or paraphrase their adversary's argument before going on to try to refute it.

We all understand the familiar straw man formula of setting up a target in order to knock it down, and how we outline the points in our brief before actually writing, but why use the crucial topic sentence or first paragraph of a major point in a brief to do your adversary's work, perhaps better and more clearly than your adversary did?

Why start a section of your brief with a restatement of your adversary's argument. Rather, state your side's argument affirmatively. Frame the question in a way that admits of only one answer — yours. Don't let your adversary define the legal issues. It becomes a crutch that is transparent, unimaginative and ineffective.

Instead of simply restating your opponents' argument, be creative and use the topic sentence to attack rather than reinforce that argument. The topic sentence in a point section of a brief is the first thing a judge will read about that argument. Use it to advantage. Regain the offensive immediately in response to your opponent's argument. Many lawyers write, at the start of, say, Point I of a brief by plaintiff, "Defendant argues that the action is barred by the statute of limitations because. . . ." This topic sentence, or something close to it, mars most briefs.

Why not begin with something like: "The action is timely. It was filed within 11 months of the incident. Defendant's argument based on the one-year statute of limitation therefore fails." This is a straightforward positive statement of *your* argument, allowing you to expand on it, and if you have to explain more of your opponent's faulty reasoning, you can do so in a subordinate placement. The suggested approach stresses why you win and your adversary loses. All it takes is a little creativity, which makes all the difference here.

SILVER BULLET 6.11. Deal with Counter-Arguments

Get the better of the major objection to your argument by raising and answering it in advance. Always offer the other side's strongest case, not the straw man. Doing so will sharpen your own argument and earn the respect of your reader. Even in your opening brief, you should deal with your adversary's anticipated counter-arguments, at least the main ones. In Justice Ginsburg's words, "You know the vulnerable points, so deal with them. Don't wait for the reply brief."

In this sense, the brief is a form of dialectic. Of course, you may want to save something for reply or lead your adversary into a trap. Bear in mind that a responsive brief does not have to follow the opponent's structure or organization. You don't have to let your adversary define the battlefield.

SILVER BULLET 6.12. Don't Make the Responsive Brief A Series of "No"s

A responsive brief has different considerations. Typically, a responsive brief is negative in the sense that it says the points in the opening brief are wrong. It is what Justice Ginsburg calls a "series of 'not sos.'" Such a negative approach has risks. The "principal danger," according to Justice Ginsburg, is that "a series of 'no's'" doesn't really work."

To avoid that trap, a lawyer can draft an answering brief even before receiving the adversary's opening brief. You can then tell your side affirmatively, and after getting the opening brief, respond to arguments you haven't dealt with.

SILVER BULLET 6.13. Use the Most Favorable Authorities

Authority matters. Use the best and most recent authorities from your court or the relevant appellate court. Avoid or at least limit string cites for well-known, uncontroversial, or obvious propositions. No one – especially a judge – likes string cites. If you use a string cite, put it in a footnote and include parentheticals fairly stating the bolding of each case.

SILVER BULLET 6.14. Deal with Contrary Authority

Do not overlook or avoid contrary authority. Cope with it as best you can. How to deal with contrary authority always poses a challenge to lawyers. First comes the threshold question of a lawyer's ethical obligation to disclose such contrary authority. But then comes the more nuanced issue of how to brush aside the adverse ruling in other cases.

We have several techniques for attempting to do so. One is to distinguish the precedent on its facts. Another is to show that the rationale behind the legal rule in the precedent has no application. Careful parsing of the precedent's operative language can help. Why is the authority no longer controlling? Changing notions of public policy — Holmes's "felt necessities of the time" — can be useful. Recall how in *MacPherson v. Buick Motor Co.*, Judge Cardozo distinguished contrary authority by saying: "Precedents drawn from the days of travel by stage coach do not fit the conditions of travel today."

The last resort is to ask a court to overturn a precedent. Keep in mind that change in the law is usually quiet and inconspicuous. American judges do not like or advertise overruling of precedents. A legal rule can be rendered obsolete by changing conditions so as to more closely correspond with social or economic facts. The hallmark of legal method is to hide or sugar coat dramatic charge. Rather than facts, the most pressing demands on law are often stability, certainty, continuity and predictability — a cluster of powerful demands militating against publicizing fundamental changes in the law. As a result American law often masks its most revolutionary changes.

Courts are reluctant to do that, and rarely do. But we all know that judges are skilled at evading (without explicitly saying so) the force of precedent when they want to. Your job is to make them want to.

SILVER BULLET 6.15. Make Conclusions Part of Your Argument

Opinion is also split on how to write a conclusion to a brief. Most conclusions in briefs essentially say no more than "we win, they lose." This is phrased slightly more elegantly as: "For the reasons given, plaintiff's motion should be denied." Some lawyers and judges favor such bare-bones conclusions, as they say precisely what the court is being asked to do.

Such bare-bones conclusions are missed opportunities. A brief is an argument. Why not finish the argument by closing powerfully, ending strong. Use the conclusion as a chance to continue your argument, much as you would in the concluding paragraph or two of an expository essay. Recapitulate your arguments and then add a few lines about the broader public policy implications of the issue, how your adversary's position is another symptom of the decline of Western Civilization, etc. Explain why the result you seek makes sense, not just in your case, but in others down the road. The point is to *use* the conclusion as something more than just a tag line:

Ex. 1

"In behaving as it did in this case, [defendant]'s management betrayed the basic tenet that people should not lose their jobs because of their political views and betrayed as well [defendant]'s contractual commitment to plaintiffs. Management also betrayed the Orchestra itself and its profound music. As [the director] tried to explain to management, the theme of much of classical repertoire is liberation and salvation through commitment to what is right, and 'Oedipus Rex' is in the same great tradition:

> The point of Oedipus Rex [one witness] explained to [Defendant's general manager]is that he tells his guards to scour the City of Thebes for the murderer of his father. And the point is after he's done trying to bully everyone else on their political points of view and . . . after the most intense introspection, he realizes the heart of these issues lies within his own self. And Thebes, the city, is destroyed by a plague, and the plague is only lifted when one man, Oedipus Rex, faces the moral imperative.

The general manager told people that [the director] was a dreamer, but in fact only [the general manager] was 'fantasi[zing].' The Music Director seemed not to care about such things; 'Fidelio', he insisted, was a 'stupid' 'story.'

"Both Oedipus and [Defendant's] management faced choices. Oedipus, unwitting of having committed any wrong, chose to face the truth in order to stop a plague. Management, although warned by [the director] that to do so would 'have serious and deadly repercussions,' chose to cancel Oedipus—both literally and figuratively—because management perceived that, in [the general manager's] words, 'the worst thing that could happen' would be for public statements to be made censuring [defendant]. Of course, it was only on odious guilt-by-association reasoning that there was anything at all censurable about [defendant's] hiring of [plaintiff] on her merits to perform in 'Oedipus Rex.' Management thus loosed a type of plague, a plague that once went by the name McCarthyism and at other times by other names, and a plague that at one time in the past almost destroyed the [defendant] itself.

"The jury tried to undo this great wrong and to stop the plague, but the trial court's rulings on the law would not allow it. This Court should reverse the profoundly dangerous rulings of law below that stood in the jury's way."

Ex. 2

"Because defendants' intentional use of a 'look-alike' and 'sound-alike' of plaintiff in their commercials is certain to cause confusion, and for all the reasons given, plaintiff's motion for a preliminary injunction should be granted. As Mr. Brimley says in his advertisements for Quaker Oats, 'It's the right thing to do.'"

Ex. 3

"Good laws can be put to bad use, which is precisely what has happened here with this antitrust class action.[Defendant], a tiny, financially struggling competitor in the model management business, has lost further economic ground in having to use its scarce resources to defend itself against unsupported charges of antitrust violations. In reality, [defendant] is being sued for one reason only: for being a member of a trade association. But that is no violation of the Sherman Act."

SILVER BULLET 6.16. The Brandeis Brief

Speaking of brief-writing, let us recall one of the most creative innovations in that genre. Louis Brandeis was a great practicing lawyer before going on the Supreme Court. One of his most important contributions to the "practice" of law was the "Brandeis brief." That audacious development was a collection of social facts rather than legal argument to educate judges about current needs.

Brandeis first used it in 1908, more than a hundred years ago. The case was *Muller v. Oregon*, which involved the constitutionality of a state law limiting to ten the number of hours a woman could work each day in a laundry. Brandeis had to come up with a way to present such a question persuasively in support of the statute. Only three years earlier, the Supreme Court had held in *Lochner v. New York* that limiting bakers' hours was unconstitutional as a violation of "liberty of contract." Rather than attack *Lochner*, Brandeis did the unexpected and transformed an apparently unfavorable precedent into a favorable one.

Here is how he did it. He cited *Lochner* as authority for a state to act where necessary to protect the health of workers, reasoning that the Supreme Court wanted more information than it got in *Lochner*. He decided to devote his brief in *Muller* almost exclusively to facts showing that long hours of manual labor for women were unhealthy. The result was an unusual two-page summary of the law and 144 pages of reports and quotations showing the relevant facts justifying the state law in question.

The Supreme Court upheld the Oregon statute and specifically noted the materials in the fact-packed Brandeis brief. It was an epoch-making creative technique that would be used again and again, and would help many years later to overthrow segregation in public schools.

Each of us can learn from Brandeis's example, and use a Brandeis-type brief when an occasion calls for it.

SILVER BULLET 6.17. The Reply Brief

Reply briefs are not required, but are almost always a good idea. It is a rare lawyer who wants or is willing to let the adversary's arguments go unanswered. Most lawyers like to have the last word. But be careful and check the applicable rules. The Federal Rules of Civil Procedure do not provide for reply briefs at the trial level, although individual judges may, and all appeal rules do.

Reply briefs have recently been taking on more importance. Judges these days often read reply briefs first, so keep that in mind when preparing them. That means you need to recap and reinforce your main arguments, not just respond to certain points made by your adversary.

In preparing a reply brief, you should ask yourself two questions. First, what questions will the court have after reading the adversary's brief?

Second, what are the biggest weaknesses — legal and factual — of each side? The answer to these questions will have great bearing on what you say in the reply brief.

Think about the order in which you want to present the arguments in your reply brief. Beware of simply using the order of your adversary's brief. To keep the court focused on what you want, you may, if it works, use the sequence of points from your opening brief. Keep control of the ball.

Within that framework, consider which points you want to respond to. Rather than correcting every factual misstatement, concentrate on material errors of fact that have an impact on the outcome. As for legal arguments, stay on the main issues of law and refute the adversary's most important arguments, while seizing the opportunity to stress again your main arguments. Deal only with your opponent's primary legal authorities, and resist the temptation to distinguish every last case cited.

Litigation being what it is, lawyers often come up with new arguments — arguments they did not think of before — by the time they are writing a reply brief. We all have that experience; if you haven't yet, you will. A reply brief, however, it not supposed to be the place for new arguments beyond responding to points raised by your opponent. Raising an issue for the first time in a reply brief is considered improper and waived. In practice, it is difficult to honor this rule when you think you have come up with a good point you missed the first time around. All I can say is be careful how you phrase it so as to avoid a court ruling it improper. Try to frame it as not being raised for the first time, but embedded or implicit in an argument previously raised in your main brief.

SEVEN

A COMIC STRIP OR
GRAPHIC NOVEL BRIEF

A shining example of creative lawyering and great, innovative brief-writing is in the Appendix. It is an actual brief filed in federal court in Manhattan in 2012. The case was a civil antitrust action brought by the U.S. Justice Department against the book publishing industry for alleged price-fixing of e-books. After the parties reached a tentative settlement, the trial judge allowed nonparties to comment on the proposed settlement, but, taking the word "brief" literally, limited the length of their submissions to only five pages. Five pages are not much space, especially in a complex antitrust case.

The brief in the Appendix is what one lawyer filed to comply with the stringent court-ordered page limit. Take a few moments to look at it and see what he did. Instead of the usual, familiar format of a legal brief, the lawyer submitted something new and different and stunningly effective: a brief in the form of a comic strip or graphic novel. He innovated. With great compression, efficiency, and clarity, coupled with an unexpected but pleasing presentation, the brief immediately catches one's attention and forcefully drives home its argument. His comic strip brief works.

It more than works. It is a remarkable, memorable achievement, a wonderful display of imaginative and creative lawyering. It complies with the court-imposed page limit by using economy of expression in a medium startlingly new for a legal brief. It makes its points with flair and a light touch in a way that is unforgettable. It simplifies the issues and, with a minimum of legal jargon, maximizes its persuasive power. It even makes the reader smile, not a common occurrence when perusing legal briefs. brilliant. It is extraordinary and amazing, even brilliant.

Like me, you will be astonished by it, will admire it, and will surely show it to other lawyers, including those in your own firm, as an example of what lawyering at its best and most creative can be.

But exactly what is it that makes this brilliant comic strip brief work so well? Its success is not simply the cliché about a picture being worth a thousand words. It is something more. Why is it so successful? The real answer is imagination and creativity in the practice of law. This comic strip brief is both fresh and effective. It surprises us, but in a good way. We look at it once and wonder, "What was he thinking?" We look at it again and say to ourselves: "Wow! Why didn't I think of that?"

This comic strip brief is a bright beacon that lights our way. It illuminates and illustrates what we practicing lawyers are capable of. It does not mean we all should now flood the courts with a tidal wave of comic strip briefs. That would not be creativity; that would be copying, with much diminished impact. But should not the rest of us, could not the rest of us, practice law with more imagination? Would not it be great if we could be more creative in our daily practice? Should we not at least try? And how do we nurture, encourage, nourish, and cultivate a cast of mind in ourselves and in our colleagues that favors imagination and creativity in our professional lives? But first we have to define what we mean by imagination and creativity.

EIGHT

CREATIVE LAWYERING

As the comic strip brief demonstrates, we should aspire to take a creative approach to our practice of law, including brief-writing. Creativity requires imagination, because imagination lets you be creative. And imagination in turn is a mysterious, hardto-explain quality, a freedom, a vision, a sense of wonder and awe, a spirit of adventure, an air of innocent merriment, a free play of the mind, a letting go, a certain puckishness, a magical, child-like ability to go beyond the ordinary. Creativity and imagination produce results both surprising and dramatic.

Imagination is what we sometimes bring, if we are lucky, to another task. Imagination improves and enhances what it is used for; it leavens anything it comes near. "Leavening" is a good way of describing imagination: imagination is the yeast that lifts any work product — including attorney work product — to a new dimension. Unleavened lawyering is like unleavened bread—matzoh—dry and unappetizing.

Leaps of creativity give us new and unexpected achievement in any field. Imagination is one of the glories of being human, perhaps even what it means to be human. "Imagination," said Albert Einstein, and he ought to know what he was talking about, "is more important than knowledge."

The practice of law does not have to be dull or boring. Creativity and the practice of law should go hand in hand. Contrary to what some people think, law should not inhibit the imagination; it should encourage it. It all depends on the lawyer, and how he or she approaches professional tasks, what attitude he or she brings to the job. There may be dull or boring lawyers, but the practice of law can be inventive and exciting. In any event, the practice of law can surely benefit from appropriate creativity and imagination.

In his 1928 book *The Paradoxes of Legal Science*, the great Benjamin Cardozo, one of our most creative judges, referred to a "kinship" between the "creative process in art" and the "creative process in law." The bridge between the two, said Cardozo, is imagination. "Imagination, whether you call it scientific or artistic, is for each the faculty that creates."

When we practice law, we have many creative moments. Choices that we make in handling a case and presenting legal arguments often turn on what Cardozo called (New York State Bar Address 1932) a "hunch," "sensation," or "intuitive flash of inspiration." The practice of law has, again in Cardozo's words (*The Paradoxes of Legal Science*), "its piercing intuitions, its tense, apocalyptic moments." That is the essence of creativity, of seeing links between apparently unrelated phenomena.

But it is creativity within limits. The practice of law circumscribes the scope of possible creativity. Just as a sonnet has 14 lines within which a poet displays imagination, so too we lawyers have certain rules, a framework, to abide by. Rules of procedure, rules of evidence, rules of ethics, and the like are our profession's equivalent of the mandatory 14 lines of a sonnet. The existence of such rules actually generates creativity within the system.

"There is emancipation in our very bonds," wrote Cardozo in *The Growth of the Law*. "The restraints of rhyme or metre, the exigencies of period or balance, liberate at times the thought which they confine, and in imprisoning release."

So why should we aspire to take a creative approach to our practice of law? Holmes gave one folksy answer in his wonderful 1897 speech "The Path of the Law." "I heard a story the other day," Holmes began, "of a man who had a valet to whom he paid high wages, subject to deduction for faults. One of his deductions was 'for lack of imagination, five dollars.'" Without expressly mentioning, but clearly implying, whom he was referring to, Holmes (probably with a wry smile and twinkling eyes) warned his audience of lawyers: "The lack [of imagination] is not confined to valets." None of us should be like that valet and be accused of lack of imagination.

Creativity is a leavening agent for what we do. It makes the practice of law more interesting and more fun. It draws on our creative impulses. It is stimulating. It adds another dimension to what we do every day, it takes our practice to another level. It makes us like creative artists, with surprising and dramatic results. It also happens to make us better lawyers and increases our chances of success. That is why we should aspire to take a creative approach to our practice of law.

But "why" is only the first inquiry. The real question is "how?" *How* can we take a creative approach to the practice of law? What specific lawyering tasks can improve with a dash of creativity? Not every case calls for a comic strip brief, but every case does require our best efforts, including our imagination. Finding those opportunities for creative lawyering is, or at least should be, our daily quest.

Legal training and practice should nourish one or more of the major components of creativity. Law does not, or at least should not, dry up one's creativity. Legal problems often call for creative solutions, and a creative individual is someone who regularly solves problems. That is what we lawyers do.

Legal thinking primarily involves logical analysis and narrative. The lawyer must obviously be skilled at arguing and giving reasons, in systematic or theoretical explanations, for this is the core of most legal reasoning and argument. A lawyer must also know how to tell a story.

The lawyer, writes Professor James Boyd White in his brilliant 1973 book *The Legal Imagination*, "lives by the power of his [or her] imagination."

The "central act of the legal mind, of judge and lawyer alike, is," says Professor White, "to tell the facts (the story) and present the legal analysis (theory) in a single work of the imagination." White goes on: "the activities that make up the professional life of the lawyer and judge constitute an enterprise of the imagination, an enterprise whose central performance is the translation of the imagination into reality by the power of language."

Since much of what we do is tell stories, we lawyers are in large part authors, with all the flexibility and artistic room that implies, limited only by facts, evidence, and ethical rules. But even subject to those professional limitations, legal storytelling is a highly creative and innovative art, and we are the artists.

Creative legal thinking depends on imaginative use of these processes. As a result of this link alone, lawyers may be conditioned for creativity. Mature and creative legal thinking must also accept uncertainty in the law, and even this uncertainty as an opportunity.

Imagination is a valuable trait in a lawyer. Whether looking for a loophole in the law, constructing a new constitutional argument, drafting an agreement, breaking a negotiating impasse, or crafting the right questions to ask a witness, imagination is important. Louis Begley, a retired corporate lawyer and prize-winning author of several highly regarded novels, says "the best and most useful lawyers are precisely the ones who are most inventive and imaginative, provided they temper invention and imagination by the exercise of good sense."

A World of Make Believe. Imagination sometimes involves pretending, and the actual practice of law can often seem to invoke a host of "let's pretend." Legal fictions, rules of evidence and rules of procedure can subordinate truth and reality in the legal hierarchy, so that courtroom truth or legal truth may not necessarily correspond to life or reality. Lawyers, in the course of advocacy, are myth-makers, as they try to make their clients seem more deserving.

Skepticism. Creative people tend to be skeptical, and reluctant to acquiesce in the findings of authority just because these have become generally accepted. Lawyers develop a skeptical attitude in general, which may enhance creativity. Experienced lawyers do not necessarily believe everything they hear from witnesses or even clients. Law school contributes to such skepticism. Scott Turow in *One L* wrote: "Thinking like a lawyer involved being suspicious and distrustful. You reevaluated statements inferred from silences, looked for loopholes and ambiguities. You did everything but take a statement at face value."

Attitude to the Past. This lawyerly skepticism generates a special and ambivalent feeling toward the past as represented by precedent. Although by temperament and training many lawyers may seem deferential to precedent, often enough they reject or at a minimum question precedent. Studying and working for years with precedents reveals their limits, and may subtly and paradoxically induce a turn of mind that yearns to rebel against the past. Those who deal all the time with precedent quickly learn not to worship it, but to manipulate it, to distinguish it, to abandon it. We point to precedent when it is helpful, but otherwise do not make a fetish of it.

Law school at its best stresses critical and creative thinking rather than rote memorization. The typical law school exam tests a student's ability to spot legal issues in a complex hypothetical fact pattern.

But enough abstract theory. How can we, how do we, apply such theory in actual practice?

Occasions for a creative approach in our practice of law are almost limitless. They arise daily, sometimes even more than once a day. From writing briefs to formulating arguments, from framing questions to presenting evidence, all such common lawyer tasks present chances for lawyerly creativity. We should recognize them and then seize them.

Your imagination is as important as your knowledge of the law.

NINE

A WORD ABOUT WORD PROCESSORS

All writing has been affected by the use of personal computers. Today most lawyers, especially younger ones, compose directly on the computer. (I do not, but that's a personal preference and a generational disability.) Using a computer to write has special benefits *and* risks, which we all need to be aware of.

On the plus side, the computer presents splendid possibilities for revision. The great value of the computer lies in its editing and revising function. Rewriting on a computer is easier than working with a typewriter. Sentences and paragraphs are a snap to move around.

On the minus side, however, writing is often made *too easy* on the computer. The computer seems to have made it possible for bad writers to write even worse. A brief ill written by hand figures, somehow, to be a bit better than a brief ill written on a word processor.

For one thing, a brief written on a word processor is likely to be longer, wordier, more garrulous generally — this owing to the ease with which words flow from the computer. The computer makes it so simple to add material; it is the great friend of second, third and even fourth thoughts on any subject. Press a few keys, manipulate the cursor, clack in a few more sentences, then watch as the paragraphs nicely reshape themselves and the brief you are working on lengthens correspondingly.

In its editing function — the ease with which nearly endless revisions can be made — lies both the joy and horror of writing on the computer. The computer lures one not to cut but to add.

Computers have changed legal research too. In many ways, computerized research has made researching the law easier and quicker and has almost done away with book research. Cases, treatises, and law review articles are available on line. But you still need the right search word. Without the key word, electronic research may be incomplete or off target.

So a word of caution. Be careful about doing legal research by computer only. Books in the law library often turn up cases and ideas for arguments missed by computerized research. Sometimes Boolean logic is not the best way to research. Sometimes a lawyer finds the right case or the right argument serendipitously as he or she flips through a reporter and sees something by chance on the page before or after the case being read. Just be careful.

TEN

TIME PRESSURE AND HOW TO DEAL WITH IT

Time management is a large part of law practice, and especially so with respect to legal writing. All this advice about legal writing and silver bullets is fine, you might say to yourself, but what about the difficult time constraints I am working under? How do I apply and follow all your advice and many hints when I am racing against the unforgiving clock? Those are fair questions.

Briefs and letters to court and adversaries do often have to be written quickly, on short deadlines, sometimes within a few days, or even overnight or in a matter of hours. As a result, rare is the litigator who has not, at least once and probably more than once, stayed up all night and, exhausted from lack of sleep, watched the sun rise just as he or she has put the finishing touches on and proofread for the last time a brief for an emergency filing or an order to show cause or responding to a temporary restraining order.

All true enough, but let's look calmly at the reality of time pressure on legal writing. Such pressure does not exist always. And when it does exist, it can usually be managed. Besides, part of being a litigator is the excitement and thrill of working under pressure. That is one reason you chose our field of practice.

Not all legal writing projects have immediate or even short deadlines. If you are the movant or appellant, you usually have plenty of lead time before filing, sometimes many months. Even if you are, say, moving to dismiss a complaint or making a discovery motion, you have weeks to prepare your papers. In most situations that is plenty of time, if one uses it properly.

Managing time properly on a legal writing project can be done. One helpful hint is not to save the actual writing to the last minute. Lawyers who routinely wait, as they may have done in college, until the night before a deadline to start writing may think they are — that night — working at white heat and rising to a higher level of consciousness in making their argument, but the reality is that such work product almost always could benefit from further thought and revision and ripening.

Start writing almost from the start of the project. In most situations, you know early on the main outlines of what you want to say, so put it down, in whatever form, on paper. Research and further thinking will refine that first draft. Waiting to write until all your research is done often creates panic and a mad dash to meet the deadline. Such a crisis is usually avoidable.

In those situations when a truly short deadline is unavoidable, the key is practice and experience and self-confidence. Whenever we learn a new skill, at first we have to consciously think carefully about each step involved. It's the same for a physical skill — riding a bike, playing golf or baseball — or a mental skill — learning how to read — at the beginning we have to concentrate on each component part and often make mistakes. But sooner or later, the task becomes second nature, we get it and do the task smoothly. Just as an experienced golfer does not consciously think about how he or she is supposed to hold his legs, arms, hands and body when swinging a golf club, so too the experienced legal writer knows what to do. The individual steps become inseparably stitched into our thinking, and muscle memory takes over.

The same process occurs with legal writing. Write enough briefs and the method become second nature. You don't think about the guidelines for good legal writing because in time you have absorbed them and they are part of your professional self. You can then produce a good legal brief under great time pressure. You'll see. Sure, it may be stressful, but if you wanted a stress-free work life, you would have chosen another line of work.

ELEVEN

HOW TO DEAL WITH AN UNRECONSTRUCTED SENIOR LAWYER, OR, IS THE SENIOR LAWYER ALWAYS RIGHT?

A practical, delicate, real-world problem awaits you. What do you do if you follow any of these writing suggestions and your boss disagrees? How do you, as a junior lawyer, handle the situation where the lawyer supervising your work is unenlightened and unreconstructed and slavishly adheres to bad legal writing habits? No doubt you have already discovered that not all the lawyers you work for will be willing to change or even be able to see the advantages of what we are all about here. Old habits die hard (cliché).

The best approach is a combination of tact, diplomacy, and waiting your turn. You have to be aware that change is difficult for almost everyone, but especially so for most lawyers, who are conservative and tradition-bound by nature and training. It is a profession that looks to precedent, and that cast of mind also applies to legal writing. If a law firm or a seasoned individual lawyer has been writing a certain way for years or even decades, he or she may not be so quick to change.

Taking all this into account, you can use some applied psychology and try to explain and demonstrate why your way is more effective in obtaining the desired objective. But your best efforts in this regard may still be unsuccessful. If so, you may find yourself in a position similar to an appellate judge who dissents. You hope that, in the fullness of time, your position will prevail. In the meantime, you have to do what the hierarchy requires and obey. In that sense, the senior lawyer is always right. It is not a question of legal ethics, so it is not worth getting fired over.

Bear in mind, and take heart, your turn will come. In a few years you will be the senior lawyer and will then be in a position to decide what rules of legal writing to follow.

TWELVE

FURTHER READING

Every lawyer should be familiar with books on writing style generally and legal writing in particular. Every lawyer should have a shelf of legal writing books. You won't agree with everything they say, but such books help develop your own distinctive legal writing style, and make you more aware of what to avoid.

In the general category, most people have their own personal favorites. *The Elements of Style* by William Strunk and E.B. White is probably the most popular and overpraised book of this type. Like a judicial opinion by Holmes or Cardozo, it is beautifully written, contains many penetrating insights, but is so general and vague that it rarely tells you how to solve a particular writing problem. "Strunk and White," as it is universally referred to, puts you in the mood for writing without supplying much concrete assistance. At least that has been my experience since a high school English teacher first made me aware of this famous little book.

Far more helpful (to me) than Strunk and White are *On Writing Well* (1980) by William Zinsser and *Simple & Direct* (1985) by Jacques Barzun. These two stylebooks tell you how to write gracefully and effectively, with many subtle, sophisticated suggestions. By all means, also read *Draft No. 4* by John McPhee, who well describes the writing process.

You should also have within easy reach a grammar book. We all have grammar questions from time to time. Grammar books, of which there are many, are, like dictionaries or encyclopedias, difficult to read cover to cover but often are fascinating to dip into or skim. Some are *Woe Is I* by

Patricia T. O'Connor (1996), *Dreyer's English* by Benjamin Dreyer (2019). Also consult *The Careful Writer* by Theodore C. Bernstein (1965).

For writing reference, you should have one of the good style manuals, such as the ones published by the New York Times, the Associated Press, or the University of Chicago. The second edition of *Fowler's Modern English Usage*, a classic, is fascinating to browse in.

But the most essential stylebooks are good ones specifically about legal writing. The best ones I know of are: *The Lawyer's Guide to Writing Well* (3rd ed. 2016) by Tom Goldstein and Jethro K. Lieberman; *Making Your Case: The Art of Persuading Judges* (4th ed. 2008) by Antonin Scalia & Bryan A. Garner; *When Lawyers Write* (1987) by Richard H. Weisberg; *The Elements of Legal Style* (1991) by Bryan A. Garner; *The Winning Brief* (1999) also by Garner; *Writing to Win* (1999) by Stephen D. Stark; *The Art of Advocacy* (2013) by Noah Messing; *Point Made* (2011) by Ross Guberman; *The 12 Secrets of Persuasive Argument* (2009) by Ronald Waicukauski, Paul Sandler & Joanne Epps; *The Legal Writer: Writing It Right* (2016) by Gerald Lebovits; and *Litigation Logic: A Practical Guide to Effective Argument* by Paul Bosanac (2009).

All these books superbly guide lawyers through the difficulties of legal writing.

A fascinating and unusual source is a 2020 collection of interviews with the Supreme Court justices published by The Scribes Journal of Legal Writing. The volume is available online at http://www.scribes.org/sites/default/files/Scribes-Journal_Volume-13_Garner-Transcripts.pdf.

If you want to write well in the law, study these books carefully. Don't let them sit on the shelf. Use them to make some of your own legal/literary silver bullets.

L'ENVOI

If you have an unbeatable case, it may not matter a damn how you write. But all the same it's better to write well than ill. The struggle to write well never ends, and the rewards are great. You will develop a love of the flavor of words and an awareness of their nuance. Legal writing can also be fun, as well as effective.

To sum up, as Somerset Maugham says in a memoir aptly called *The Summing Up*, "If you could write lucidly, simply, euphoniously and yet with liveliness, you would write perfectly." That is our aspirational goal.

You will near that goal when judges, adversaries, colleagues, and clients admire your written work enough to change the question posed by those helped by the Lone Ranger ("Who was that masked man?) to "Who wrote that brief?" Then your legal writing will have become your silver bullet.

APPENDIX

IN THE UNITED STATES DISTRICT COURT
FOR THE SOUTHERN DISTRICT OF NEW YORK

UNITED STATES OF AMERICA)
)
Plaintiff,)
)
v.)   Civil Action No.12-CV-2826 (DLC)
)
APPLE, INC.,)
HACHETTE BOOK GROUP, INC.,)
HARPERCOLLINS PUBLISHERS, L.L.C.)
VERLAGSGRUPPE GEORG VON)
HOLTZBRINK PUBLISHERS, LLC)
    d/b/a MACMILLAN,)
THE PENGUIN GROUP,)
    A DIVISION OF PEARSON PLC,)
PENGUIN GROUP (USA), INC. and)
SIMON & SCHUSTER, INC.,)
)
Defendants.)

BRIEF OF BOB KOHN AS *AMICUS CURIAE* [*]

---

[*] Five-page version of Proposed Brief *Amicus Curiae* at Docket No. 97.

Dated: September 4, 2012

Respectfully submitted,

BOB KOHN

BOB KOHN
(California Bar No. 100793)
140 E. 28th St.
New York, NY 10016
+1-408-602-5646
bob@bobkohn.com

www.ingramcontent.com/pod-product-compliance
Lightning Source LLC
Chambersburg PA
CBHW021502210526
45463CB00002B/850